R. Charlton Mitchell

Extracts from the Army Regulations

For the use of the non-commissioned officers and soldiers of the fifty-first

regiment, N.Y.V.

R. Charlton Mitchell

Extracts from the Army Regulations
For the use of the non-commissioned officers and soldiers of the fifty-first regiment,
N.Y.V.

ISBN/EAN: 9783337308872

Printed in Europe, USA, Canada, Australia, Japan

Cover: Foto ©ninafisch / pixelio.de

More available books at **www.hansebooks.com**

EXTRACTS

FROM

"THE ARMY REGULATIONS,"

FOR THE USE OF

THE NON-COMMISSIONED OFFICERS AND SOLDIERS OF THE FIFTY-FIRST REGIMENT N. Y. V.

COMPILED BY R. CHARLTON MITCHELL,

Captain Fifty-first Regiment N. Y. V.

BY ORDER OF

COL. EDWARD FERRERO,

COMMANDING.

ANNAPOLIS.
ELIHU S. RILEY, PRINTER.
1861.

NON-COMMISSIONED OFFICERS AND
SOLDIERS OF THE 51st REG., N. Y. V:

This little work has been compiled for your use, by order of your Colonel, in it, you will find such extracts from the "Army Regulations," and "Articles of War," as relate to your duties as soldiers. The Colonel, in placing a copy of it, in the hands of each of you, trusts that you will not only *read*, but *study* it, and endeavor, in every way, to conform to the line of duty it lays down for you.

R. C. M.

i

EXTRACTS

FROM

THE ARMY REGULATIONS.

MILITARY DISCIPLINE.

1. All inferiors are required to obey strictly, and to execute with alacrity and good faith, the lawful orders of the superiors appointed over them.

COMPANIES.

89. The name of each soldier will be labeled on his bunk, and his company number will be placed against his arms and accoutrements.

90. The arms will be placed in the arm-racks, the stoppers in the muzzles, the cocks let down, and the bayonets in their scabbards; the accoutrements suspended over the arms, and the swords hung up by the belts on pegs.

91. The knapsack of each man will be placed on the lower shelf of his bunk, at its foot, packed with his effects, and ready to be slung; the great-coat on the same shelf, rolled and strapped; the coat, folded inside out, and placed under the knapsack; the cap on the second or upper shelf; and the boots well cleaned.

92. Dirty clothes will be kept in an appropriate part of the knap-sack; no article of any kind to be put under the bedding.

93. Cooking utensils and table equipage will be cleaned and arranged in closets or recesses; blacking and brushes out of view; the fuel in boxes.

94. Ordinarily the cleaning will be on Saturdays. The

chiefs of squads will cause bunks and bedding to be over-hauled; floors dry rubbed; tables and benches scoured; arms cleaned; accoutrements whitened and polished, and everything put in order.

95. Where conveniences for bathing are to be had, the men should bathe once a week. The feet to be washed at least twice a week. The hair *kept short*, and beard neatly trimmed.

96. Non-commissioned officers, in command of squads, will be held more immediately responsible that their men observe what is prescribed above; that they wash their hands and faces daily; that they brush or comb their heads; that those who are to go on duty put their arms, accoutrements, dress, &c., in the best order, and that such as have permission to pass the chain of sentinels are in the dress that may be ordered.

97. Commanders of companies and squads will see that the arms and accoutrements in possession of the men are always kept in good order, and that proper care be taken in cleaning them.

98. When belts are given to a soldier, the captain will see that they are properly fitted to the body; and it is forbidden to cut any belt without his sanction.

99. Cartridge-boxes and bayonet-scabbards will be polished with blacking; varnish is injurious to the leather, and will not be used.

100. All arms in the hands of the troops, whether browned or bright, will be kept in the state in which they are issued by the Ordnance Department. Arms will not be taken to pieces without permission of a commissioned officer. Bright barrels will be kept clean and free from rust without polishing them; care should be taken in rubbing not to bruise or bend the barrel. After firing, wash out the bore; wipe it dry, and then pass a bit of cloth, slightly greased, to the bottom. In these operations, a rod of wood with a loop in one end is to be used instead of the rammer. The barrel, when not in use, will be closed with a stopper. For exercise, each soldier should keep himself provided with a piece of sole leather to fit the cup or countersink of the hammer.

101. Arms shall not be left loaded in quarters or tents, or when the men are off duty, except by special orders.

102. Ammunition issued will be inspected frequently. Each man will be made to pay for the rounds expended without orders, or not in the way of duty, or which may be damaged or lost by his neglect.

103. Ammunition will be frequently exposed to the dry air, or sunned.

104. Special care shall be taken to ascertain that no ball-

cartridges are mixed with the blank cartridges issued to the men.

105. All knapsacks are to be painted black. Those for the artillery will be marked in the centre of the cover with the number of the regiment only, in figures of one inch and a half in length, of the character called full face, with yellow paint. Those for the infantry will be marked in the same way, in white paint. Those for the ordnance will be marked with two cannon, crossing; the cannon to be seven and a half inches in length, in yellow paint, to resemble those on the cap. The knapsack straps will be black.

106. The knapsacks will also be marked upon the inner side with the letter of the company and the number of the soldier, on such part as may be readily observed at inspections.

107. Haversacks will be marked upon the flap with the number and name of the regiment, the letter of the company, and number of the soldier, in black letters and figures. And each soldier must, at all times, be provided with a haversack and canteen, and will exhibit them at all inspections. It will be worn on the left side on marches, guard, and when paraded for detached service—the canteen outside the haversack.

108. The front of the drums will be painted with the arms of the United States, on a blue field for the infantry, and on a red field for the artillery. The letter of the company and number of the regiment, under the arms, in a scroll.

110. Soldiers will wear the prescribed uniform in camp or garrison, and will not be permitted to keep in their possession any other clothing. When on fatigue parties, they will wear the proper fatigue dress.

225. Immediately after *reveille* roll-call, the tents or quarters, and the space around them, will be put in order by the men of the companies, superintended by the chiefs of squads, and the guard-house or guard-tent by the guard or prisoners.

SALUTES.

244. Courtesy among military men is indispensable to discipline. Respect to superiors will not be confined to obedience on duty, but will be extended to all occasions. It is always the duty of the inferior to accost or to offer first the customary salutation, and of the superior to return such complimentary notice.

245. Sergeants, with swords drawn, will salute by bring-

ing them to a present—with muskets, by bringing the left hand across the body, so as to strike the musket near the right shoulder. Corporals out of the ranks, and privates not sen-'tries, will carry their muskets at a shoulder as sergeants, and salute in like manner.

246. When a soldier without arms, or with side-arms only, meets an officer, he is to raise his hand to the right side of the visor of his cap, palm to the front, elbow raised as high as the shoulder, looking at the same time in a respectful and soldier-like manner at the officer, who will return the compliment thus offered.

247. A non-commissioned officer or soldier being seated, and without particular occupation, will rise on the approach of an officer, and make the customary salutation. If standing, he will turn toward the officer for the same purpose. If the parties remain in the same place or on the same ground, such compliments need not be repeated.

GUARDS AND DUTIES OF SENTINELS.

389. Sentinels will be relieved every two hours, unless the state of the weather, or other causes, should make it necessary or proper that it be done at shorter or longer intervals.

390. Each relief, before mounting, is inspected by the commander of the guard or of its post. The Corporal reports to him, and presents the old relief on its return.

391. The *countersign*, or watchword, is given to such per-.ons as are entitled to pass during the night, and to officers. non-commissioned officers, and sentinels of the guard Interior guards receive the countersign only when ordered by the commander of the troops.

392. The *parole* is imparted to such officers only as have a right to visit the guards, and to make the grand rounds ; and to officers commanding guards.

393. As soon as the new guard has been marched off, the officer of the day will repair to the office of the commanding officer and report for orders.

394. The officer of the day must see that the officer of the guard is furnished with the parole and countersign before *retreat.*

395. The officer of the day visits the guards during the day at such times as he may deem necessary, and makes his rounds at night at least once after 12 o'clock.

396. Upon being relieved, the officer of the day will make

such remarks in the report of the officer of the guard as circumstances require, and present the same at head-quarters.

397. Commanders of guards leaving their posts to visit their sentinels, or on other duty, are to mention their intention, and the probable time of their absence, to the next in command.

398. The officers are to remain constantly at their guards, except while visiting their sentinels, or necessarily engaged elsewhere on their proper duty.

399. Neither officers nor soldiers are to take off their clothing or accoutrements while they are on guard.

400. The officer of the guard must see that the countersign is duly communicated to the sentinels a little before twilight.

401. When a fire breaks out, or any alarm is raised in a garrison all guards are to be immediately under arms.

402. Inexperienced officers are put on guard as supernumeraries, for the purpose of instruction.

403. Sentinels will not take orders or allow themselves to be relieved, except by an officer or non-commissioned officer of their guard or party, the officer of the day, or the commanding officer; in which case the orders will be immediately notified to the commander of the guard by the officer giving them.

404. Sentinels will report every breach of orders or regulations they are instructed to enforce.

405. Sentinels must keep themselves on the alert, observing every thing that takes place within sight and hearing of their post. They will carry their arms habitually at support, or on either shoulder, but will never quit them. In wet weather, if there be no sentry-box, they will secure arms.

406. No sentinel shall quit his post or hold conversation not necessary to the proper discharge of his duty.

407. All persons, of whatever rank in the service, are required to observe respect toward sentinels.

408. In case of disorder, a sentinel must call out *the guard;* and if a fire take place, he must cry—*"Fire!"* adding the number of his post. If in either case the danger be great, he must discharge his firelock before calling out.

409. It is the duty of a sentinel to repeat all calls made from posts more distant from the main body of the guard than his own, and no sentinel will be posted so distant as not to be heard by the guard, either directly or through other sentinels.

410. Sentinels will present arms to general and field officers, to the officer of the day, and to the commanding officer of the post. To all other officers they will carry arms.

411. When a sentinel in his sentry-box sees an officer approaching ap-

2

proaching, he will stand at *attention*, and as the officer passes will salute him, by bringing the left hand briskly to the musket, as high as the right shoulder.

412. The sentinel at any post of the guard, when he sees any body of troops, or an officer entitled to compliment, approach, must call—*"Turn out the guard!"* and announce who approaches.

413. Guards do not turn out as a matter of compliment after sunset; but sentinels will, when officers in uniform approach, pay them proper attention, by facing to the proper front, and standing steady at *shouldered arms*. This will be observed until the evening is so far advanced that the sentinels begin challenging.

414. After retreat (or the hour appointed by the commanding officer), until broad daylight, a sentinel challenges every person who approaches him, taking, at the same time, the position of *arms port*. He will suffer no person to come nearer than within reach of his bayonet, until the person has given the countersign.

415. A sentinel, in challenging, will call out—*"Who comes there?"* If answered—*"Friend, with the countersign,"* and he be instructed to pass persons with the countersign, he will reply—*"Advance, friend, with the countersign!"* If answered—*"Friends!"* he will reply—*"Halt, friends! Advance one with the countersign!"* If answered—*"Relief,"* *"Patrol,"* or *"Grand Rounds,"* he will reply—*"Halt, Advance, Sergeant (or Corporal), with the countersign!"* and satisfy himself that the party is what it represents itself to be. If he have no authority to pass persons with the countersign, if the wrong countersign be given, or if the persons have not the countersign, he will cause them to stand, and call—*"Corporal of the guard!"*

416. In the day time, when the sentinel before the guard sees the officer of the day approach, he will call—*"Turn out the guard! officer of the day."* The guard will be paraded, and salute with presented arms.

417. When any person approaches a post of the guard at night, the sentinel before the post, after challenging, causes him to halt until examined by a non-commissioned officer of the guard. If it be the officer of the day, or any other officer entitled to inspect the guard and to make the rounds, the non-commissioned officer will call—*"Turn out the guard!"* when the guard will be paraded at shouldered arms, and the officer of the guard, if he thinks necessary, may demand the countersign and parole.

418. The officer of the day, wishing to make the rounds, will take an escort of a non-commissioned officer and two

men. When the rounds are challenged by a sentinel, the Sergeant will answer—*"Grand Rounds,"* and the sentinel will reply—*"Halt, Grand rounds! Advance, Sergeant, with the countersign."* Upon which the Sergeant advances and gives the countersign. The sentinel will then cry—*"Advance rounds!"* and stand at a shoulder till they have passed.

419. When the sentinel before the guard challenges, and is answered—*"Grand rounds,"* he will reply—*"Halt, grand rounds! Turn out the guard; grand rounds!"* Upon which the guard will be drawn up at shouldered arms. The officer commanding the guard will then order a Sergeant and two men to advance; when within ten paces, the Sergeant challenges. The Sergeant of the grand rounds answers—*"Grand rounds!"* The Sergeant of the guard replies—*"Advance, Sergeant, with the countersign!"* The Sergeant of the rounds advances alone, gives the countersign, and returns to his round. The Sergeant of the guard calls to his officer—*"The countersign is right!"* on which the officer of the guard calls —*"Advance, rounds!"* The officer of the rounds then advances alone, the guard standing at shouldered arms. The officer of the rounds passes along the front of the guard to the officer, who keeps his post on the right, and gives him the parole. He then examines the guard, orders back his escort, and, taking a new one, proceeds in the same manner to other guards.

420. All material instructions given to a sentinel on post by persons entitled to make grand rounds, ought to be promptly notified to the commander of the guard.

421. Any General officer, or the commander of a post or garrison, may visit the guards of his command, and go the grand rounds, and be received in the same manner as prescribed for the officer of the day.

——————

POLICE GUARD.

569. The police guard and the advanced post pay the same honors as others guards. They take arms when an armed body approaches.

570. The sentinel over the colors has orders not to permit them to be moved except in presence of an escort; to let no one touch them but the color-bearer, or the sergeant of the police guard when he is accompanied by two armed men.

571. The sentinels on the color front permit no soldier to take arms from the stacks, except by order of some officer, or

a non-commissioned officer of the guard. The sentinel at the Colonel's tent has orders to warn him, day or night, of any unusual movement in or about the camp.

572. The sentinels on the front, flanks, and rear, see that no soldier leaves camp with horse or arms unless conducted by a non-commissioned officer. They prevent non-commissioned officers and soldiers from passing out at night, except to go to the sinks, and mark if they return. They arrest, at any time, suspicious persons prowling about the camp, and at night, every one who attempts to enter, even the soldiers of other corps. Arrested persons are sent to the officer of the guard, who sends them, if necessary, to the officer of the day.

573. The sentinels on the front of the advanced post have orders to permit neither non-commissioned officers nor soldiers to pass the line, without reporting at the advanced post ; to warn the advanced post of the approach of any armed body, and to arrest all suspicious persons. The sergeant sends persons so arrested to the officer of the guard, and warns him of the approach of any armed body.

574. The sentinel over the arms at the advanced post guards the prisoners and keeps sight of them, *and suffers no one to converse with them without permission.* They are only permitted to go to the sinks one at a time, and under a sentinel.

575. If any one is to be passed out of camp at night, the officer of the guard sends him under an escort to the advanced post, and the sergeant of the post has him passed over the chain.

576. At retreat, the officer of the guard has the roll of his guard called, and inspects arms, to see that they are loaded and in order ; and visits the advanced post for the same purpose. The sergeant of the police guard, accompanied by two armed soldiers, folds the colors and lays them on the trestle in rear of the arms. He sees that the sutler's stores are then closed, and the men leave them, and that the kitchen fires are put out at the appointed hour.

PLUNDERING.

768. Plundering and marauding, at all times disgraceful to soldiers, when committed on the persons or property of those whom it is the duty of the army to protect, become crimes of such enormity as to admit of no remission of the awful punishment which the military law awards against offenses of this nature.

TROOPS ON BOARD OF TRANSPORTS.

834. Immediately after embarking, the men will be assigned to quarters, equal parties on each side of the ship, *and no man will be allowed to loiter or sleep on the opposite side.* As far as practicable, the men of each company will be assigned to the same part of the vessel, and the squads, in the same manner, to contiguous berths.

835. Arms will be so placed, if there be no racks, as to be secure from injury, and enable the men to handel them promptly—bayonets unfixed and in scabbard.

838. The guard will be proportioned to the number of sentinels required. At sea the guard will mount with side-arms only. The officer of the guard will be officer of the day.

839. Sentinels will be kept over the fires, with buckets of water at hand, promptly to extinguish fires. Smoking is prohibited *between decks or in the cabins,* at all times; nor shall any lights be allowed between decks, except such ship lanterns as the master of the transport may direct, or those carried by the officer of the day in the execution of his duty.

840. Regulations will be adopted to enable companies or messes to cook in turn ; no others than those whose turn it is, will be allowed to loiter around or approach the galleys or other cooking places.

842. All the troops will turn out at ——, A. M. without arms or uniform, and (in warm weather) without shoes or stockings ; when every individual will be clean, his hands, face, and feet washed, and his hair combed. The same personal inspection will be repeated thirty minutes before sunset. The cooks alone may be exempted from *one* of these inspections per day, if necessary.

843. Recruits or awkward men will be exercised in the morning and evening in the use of arms, an hour each time, when the weather will permit.

844. Officers will enforce cleanliness as indispensable to health. When the weather will permit, bedding will be brought on deck every morning for airing. Tubs may be fixed on the forecastle for bathing, or the men may be placed in the *chains* and have buckets of water thrown over them.

847. During cooking hours, the officers of companies visit the camboose, and see that the messes are well prepared. The copppers and other cooking utensils are to be regularly and well washed, both *before* and *after* use.

848. The bedding will be replaced in the berths at sunset, or at an earlier hour when there is a prospect of bad weather and at *tattoo* every man not on duty will be in his berth.

EXTRACTS FROM THE ARTICLES OF WAR.

AN ACT FOR ESTABLISHING RULES AND ARTICLES FOR THE GOVERN-
MENT OF THE ARMIES OF THE UNITED STATES.

SECTION 1. *Be it enacted, by the Senate and House of Repre-
sentatives of the United States of America, in Congress assem-
bled,* That, from and after the passing of this act, the following shall be the rules and articles by which the armies of the
United States shall be governed.

ART. 2. It is earnestly recommended to all officers and soldiers diligently to attend divine service; and all officers who
shall behave indecently or irreverently at any place of divine
worship shall, if commissioned officers, be brought before a
general court-martial, there to be publicly and severely repri-
manded by the president; if non-commissioned officers or soldiers, every person so offending shall, for his first offense, forfeit one sixth of a dollar, to be deducted out of his next pay;
for the second offense, he shall not only forfeit a like sum,
but be confined twenty-four hours; and for every like offense, shall suffer and pay in like manner; which money, so
forfeited, shall be applied, by the captain or senior officer of
the troop or company, to the use of the sick soldiers of the
company or troop to which the offender belongs.

ART. 3. Any non-commissioned officer or soldier who shall
use any profane oath or execration, shall incur the penalties
expressed in the foregoing article; and a commissioned officer
shall forfeit and pay, for each and every such offense, one
dollar, to be applied as in the preceeding article.

ART. 5. Any officer or soldier who shall use contemptuous
or disrespectful words against the President of the United
States, against the Vice-President thereof, against the Congress of the United States, or against the Chief Magistrate or
Legislature of any of the United States, in which he may be quar-
tered, if a commissioned officer, shall be cashiered, or otherwise punished, as a court-martial shall direct; if a non-commissioned officer or soldier, he shall suffer such punishment
as shall be inflicted on him by the sentence of a court-martial.

ART. 6. Any officer or soldier who shall behave himself
with contempt or disrespect toward his commanding officer,
shall be punished, according to the nature of his offence, by
the judgment of a court-martial.

ART. 7. Any officer or soldier who shall begin, excite,

cause, or join in, any mutiny or sedition, in any troop or company in the service of the United States, or in any party, post, detachment, or guard, shall suffer death, or such other punishment as by a court-martial shall be inflicted.

ART. 8. Any officer, non-commissioned officer, or soldier, who, being present at any mutiny or sedition, does not use his utmost endeavor to suppress the same, or, coming to the knowledge of any intended mutiny, does not, without delay, give information thereof to his commanding officer, shall be punished by the sentence of a court-martial with death, or otherwise, according to the nature of his offense.

ART. 9. Any officer or soldier who shall strike his superior officer, or draw or lift up any weapon, or offer any violence against him, being in the execution of his office, on any pretense whatsoever, or shall disobey any lawful command of his superior officer, shall suffer death, or such other punishment as shall, according to the nature of his offense, be inflicted upon him by the sentence of a court-martial.

ART. 20. All officers and soldiers who have received pay, or have been duly enlisted in the service of the United States, and shall be convicted of having deserted the same, shall suffer death, or such other punishment as, by sentence of a court-martial, shall be inflicted.

ART. 21. Any non-commissioned officer or soldier who shall, without leave from his commanding officer, absent himself from his troop, company, or detachment, shall, upon being convicted thereof, be punished according to the nature of his offense, at the discretion of a court-martial.

ART. 22. No non-commissioned officer or soldier shall enlist himself in any other regiment, troop, or company, without a regular discharge from the regiment, troop, or company in which he last served, on the penalty of being reputed a deserter, and suffering accordingly. And in case any officer shall knowingly receive and entertain such non-commissoned officer or soldier, or shall not, after his being discovered to be a deserter, immediately confine him, and give notice thereof to the corps in which he last served, the said officer shall, by a court-martial, be cashiered.

ART. 23. Any officer or soldier who shall be convicted of having advised or persuaded any other officer or soldier to desert the service of the United States, shall suffer death, or such other punishment as shall be inflicted upon him by the sentence of a court-martial.

ART. 24. No officer or soldier shall use any reproachful or provoking speeches or gestures to another, upon pain, if an officer, of being put in arrest; if a soldier, confined, and of

asking pardon of the party offended, in the presence of his commanding officer.

ART. 25. No officer or soldier shall send a challenge to another officer or soldier, to fight a duel, or accept a challenge if sent, upon pain, if a commissioned officer, of being cashiered ; if a non-commissioned officer or soldier, of suffering corporeal punishment, at the discretion of a court-martial.

ART. 26. If any commissioned or non-commissioned officer commanding a guard shall knowingly or willingly suffer any person whatsoever to go forth to fight a duel, he shall be punished as a challenger; and all seconds, promoters, and carriers of challenges, in order to duels, shall be deemed principals, and be punished accordingly. And it shall be the duty of every officer commanding an army, regiment, company, post, or detachment, who is knowing to a challenge being given or accepted by any officer, non-commissioned officer, or soldier, under his command, or has reason to believe the same to be the case, immediately to arrest and bring to trial such offenders.

ART. 27. All officers, of what condition soever, have power to part and quell all quarrels, frays, and disorders, though the persons concerned should belong to another regiment, troop, or company : and either to order officers into arrest, or non-commissioned officers or soldiers into confinement, until their proper superior officers shall be acquainted therewith ; and whosoever shall refuse to obey such officer (though of an inferior rank), or shall draw his sword upon him, shall be punished at the discretion of a general court-martial.

ART. 28. Any officer cr soldier who shall upraid another for refusing a challenge, shall himself be punished as a challenger ; and all officers and soldiers are hereby discharged from any disgrace or opinion of disadvantage which might arise from their having refused to accept of challenges, as they will only have acted in obedience to the laws, and done their duty as good soldiers who subject themselves to discipline.

ART. 35. If any inferior officer or soldier shall think himself wronged by his Captain or other officer, he is to complain thereof to the commanding officer of the regiment, who is hereby required to summon a regimental court-martial, for the doing justice to the complainant ; from which regimental court-martial either party may, if he thinks himself still aggrieved, appeal to a general court-martial. But if, upon a second hearing, the appeal shall appear vexatious and groundless, the person so appealing shall be punished at the discretion of the said court-martial.

3

ART. 36. Any commissioned officer, store-keeper, or commissary, who shall be convicted at a general court-martial of having sold, without a proper order for that purpose, embezzled, misapplied, or willfully, or through neglect, suffered any of the provisions, forage, arms, clothing, ammunition, or other military stores belonging to the United States to be spoiled or damaged, shall, at his own expense, make good the loss or damage, and shall, moreover, forfeit all his pay, and be dismised from the service.

ART. 37. Any non-commissioned officer or soldier who shall be convicted at a regimental court-martial of having sold, or designedly or through neglect, wasted the ammunition delivered out to him, to be employed in the service of the United States, shall be punished at the discretion of such court.

ART. 38. Every non-commissioned officer or soldier who shall be convicted before a court-martial of having sold, lost, or spoiled, through neglect, his horse, arms, clothes, or accoutrements, shall undergo such weekly stoppages (not exceeding the half of his pay) as such court-martial shall judge sufficient, for repairing the loss or damage; and shall suffer confinement, or such other corporeal punishment as his crime shall deserve.

ART. 39. Every officer who shall be convicted before a court-martial of having embezzled or misapplied any money with which he may have been intrusted, for the payment of the men under his command, or for enlisting men into the service, or for other purposes, if a commissioned officer, shall be cashiered, and compelled to refund the money; if a non-commissioned officer, shall be reduced to the ranks, be put under stoppages until the money be made good, and suffer such corporeal punishment as such court-martial shall direct.

ART. 41. All non-commissioned officers and soldiers who shall be found one mile from the camp without leave, in writing, from their commanding officer, shall suffer such punishment as shall be inflicted upon them by the sentence of a court-martial.

ART. 42. No officer or soldier shall lie out of his quarters, garrison, or camp without leave from his superior officer, upon penalty of being punished according to the nature of his offense, by the sentence of a court-martial.

ART. 43. Every non-commissioned officer and soldier shall retire to his quarters or tent at the beating of the retreat; in default of which he shall be punished according to the nature of his offense.

ART. 44. No officer, non-commissioned officer, or soldier shall fail in repairing, at the time fixed, to the place of pa-

rade, of exercise, or other rendezvous appointed by his commanding officer, if not prevented by sickness or some other evident necessity, or shall go from the said place of rendezvous without leave from his commanding officer, before he shall be regularly dismissed or relieved, on the penalty of being punished, according to the nature of his offense, by the sentence of a court-martial.

ART. 45. Any commissioned officer who shall be found drunk on his guard, party, or other duty, shall be cashiered. Any non-commissioned officer or soldier so offending shall suffer such corporeal punishment as shall be inflicted by the sentence of a court-martial.

ART. 46. Any sentinel who shall be found sleeping upon his post, or shall leave it before he shall be regularly relieved, shall suffer death, or such other punishment as shall be inflicted by the sentence of a court-martial.

ART. 47. No soldier belonging to any regiment, troop, or company shall hire another to do his duty for him, or be excused from duty but in cases of sickness, disability, or leave of absence; and every such soldier found guilty of hiring his duty, as also the party so hired to do another's duty, shall be punished at the discretion of a regimental court-martial.

ART. 48. And every non-commissioned officer conniving at such hiring of duty aforesaid, shall be reduced; and every commissioned officer knowing and allowing such ill practices in the service, shall be punished by the judgment of a general court.martial.

ART. 50. Any officer or soldier who shall, without urgent necessity, or without the leave of his superior officer, quit his guard, platoon, or division, shall be punished, according to the nature of his offense, by the sentence of a court-martial.

ART. 51. No officer or soldier shall do violence to any person who brings provision or other necessaries to the camp, garrison, or quarters of the forces of the United States, employed in any parts out of the said States, upon pain of death, or such other punishment as a court-martial shall direct.

ART. 52. Any officer or soldier who shall misbehave himself before the enemy, run away, or shamefully abandon any fort, post, or guard which he or they may be commanded to defend, or speak words inducing others to do the like, or shall cast away his arms and ammunition, or who shall quit his post or colors to plunder and pillage, every such offender, being duly convicted thereof, shall suffer death, or such other punishment as shall be ordered by the sentence of a general court-martial.

ART. 53. Any person belonging to the armies of the United

States who shall make known the watchword to any person who is not entitled to receive it according to the rules and discipline of war, or shall presume to give a parole or watchword different from what he received, shall suffer death, or such other punishment as shall be ordered by the sentence of a general court-martial.

ART. 54. All officers and soldiers are to behave themselves orderly in quarters and on their march ; and whoever shall commit any waste or spoil, either in walks of trees, parks warrens, fish-ponds, houses, or gardens, corn-fields, inclosure, of meadows, or shall maliciously destroy any property whatsoever belonging to the inhabitants of the United States, unless by order of the then commander-in-chief of the armies of the said States, shall (besides such penalties as they are liable to by law), be punished according to the nature and degree of the offense, by the judgment of a regimental or general court-martial.

ART. 55. Whosoever, belonging to the armies of the United States in foreign parts, shall force a safeguard, shall suffer death.

ART. 56. Whosoever shall relieve the enemy with money, victuals, or ammunition, or shall knowingly harbor or protect an enemy, shall suffer death, or such other punishment as shall be ordered by the sentence of a court-martial.

ART. 57. Whosoever shall be convicted of holding correspondence with, or giving intelligence to, the enemy, either directly or indirectly, shall suffer death, or such other punishment as shall be ordered by the sentence of a court-martial.

ART. 59. If any commander of any garrison, fortress, or post shall be compelled, by the officers and soldiers under his command, to give up to the enemy, or to abandon it, the commissioned officers, non-commissioned officers, or soldiers who shall be convicted of having so offended, shall suffer death, or such other punishment as shall be inflicted upon them by the sentence of a court-martial.

ART. 60. All sutlers and retainers to the camp, and all persons whatsoever, serving with the armies of the United States in the field, though not enlisted soldiers, are to be subject to orders, according to the rules and discipline of war.

ART. 76. No person whatsoever shall use any menacing words, signs, or gestures, in presence of a court-martial, or shall cause any disorder or riot, or disturb their proceedings, on the penalty of being punished at the discretion of the said court-martial.

ART. 97. The officers and soldiers of any troops, *whether militia or others*, being mustered and in pay of the United States, shall, at all times and in all places, when joined, or acting in conjunction with the regular forces of the United States, be governed by these rulss and articles of war, and shall be subject to be tried by courts-martial, in like manner with the officers and soldiers in the regular forces ; save only that such courts-martial shall be composed entirely of militia officers.

ART. 99. All crimes not capital, and all disorders and neglects which officers and soldiers may be guilty of, to the prejudice of good order and military discipline, though not mentioned in the foregoing articles of war, are to be taken cognizance of by a general or regimental court-martial, according to the nature and degree of the offense, and be punished at their discretion.

APPENDIX.

As much of the sickness incident to Camp life, is due to improperly cooked food, the following admirable directions for cooking Soldiers' Rations, taken from "Vielle's Handbook for Active Service," are particularly recommended to the attention of both non-commissioned officers and soldiers.

RECEIPTS.

1st.—*Soldier's Soup for* 25 *men.*

15 quarts of water to 25 pounds of meat, 2 small table-spoonsful of salt, half a one of pepper, about 2 pounds of rice put in while boiling, and what vegetables, fresh or preserved, that can be procured—say 3 pounds.

2nd.—*Pork Soup for* 25 *men.*

In 6 gallons of cold water put 12 pounds of pork, 3 quarts of beans, 2 pounds of rice, season to suit ; let boil one hour and a half. Soak the beans over night.

3d.—*Irish Stew for* 25 *men.*

25 pounds of mutton, veal, beef or pork, cut into pieces six inches square, four pounds of onions, 8 pounds potatoes, 4 table-spoonsful of salt, 1 of pepper ; add 8 quarts of water. Cook it from one to two hours slowly, thicken the gravy with flour mixed into a smooth paste with water, or potatoes mashed fine.

4th.—*Tea for* 25 *men.*

Allow 12 quarts of water ; put the rations of tea—a large teaspoonful to each—in a cloth tied up very loosely, throw it into the boiler while it is boiling hard for a moment. Then

take off the boiler, cover it and let it stand full ten minutes, when it will be ready to use; first add sugar and milk, if to be had, at the rate of 3 pints or 2 quarts of milk and a pound or a pound and a half of sugar.

5th.—Pork with Peas or Beans for 25 men.

To 14 pounds of pork add 6 pounds of peas or beans, put them in a cloth to boil, tying it very loosely, place them both in the boiler; let them boil about two hours. Then take out the pork, add some flour to the gravy, and put the peas or beans in it with two or three onions cut up fine; let it boil a little longer, mash up the vegetables very finely and serve them round the dish with the meat.

6th.—Plain stewed Meat for 25 men.

Take 14 pounds of mutton, beef, veal, or pork, cut it into chunks and put it in the boiler. Add 4 quarts of water, 2 quarts to a teaspoonful of salt, and half a teaspoonful of pepper, 8 or 10 onions cut in pieces; let it boil half an hour, then let it stew slowly from half an hour to an hour longer, adding 1 pound of rice, potatoes or any vegetable that can be obtained; thicken the gravy with flour mixed to a smooth paste in cold water.

7th.—Stewed Salt Pork or Beef for 25 men.

Wash the meat well, let it soak all night, wash out the salt as much as possible; 8 pounds of salt Beef, 5 pounds of salt Pork, $\frac{1}{3}$ of a pound of sugar, two pounds of sliced onions, 6 quarts of water and a pound of rice; let it simmer gently for two or three hours.

8th.—Salt Pork, with Potatoes and Cabbage for 25 men.

Take 15 pounds of pork, extract the bones, 3 pounds of potatoes, 2 winter cabbages, 10 quarts of water, let it boil for two hours. Serve the meat with vegetables round it. The gravy will make a good broth with peas, beans or rice added, also a little onion. Ship biscuit broken into the broth makes a very nutritious soup.

9th.—Coffee for 25 men.

Take 12 quarts of water, when it boils add 20 ounces of coffee, mix it well and leave it on the fire till it commences to boil; then take it off and pour into it a little more than a quart of cold water; let it stand in a warm place full ten minutes; the dregs will settle at the bottom and the coffee be perfectly clear; pour it then into another vessel leaving the dregs in the first: add sugar 4 teaspoonfuls to the quart. If

you can get milk, leave out five quarts of water in the above receipt, and put milk in its place.

10th.—*Peas or Bean Soup for 25 men.* ·

·Take 14 pounds of pork, 8 quarts of peas or beans, 20 quarts of water, 25 teaspoonfuls of sugar, 12 of pepper, and several large onions, boil gently till the vegetables are soft, from four to five hours.

11th.—*Receipt for a small quantity of mashed meat.*

.Cut the meat in very small pieces; heat the frying pan, put into it half a pint of water, half a tea spoonful of salt, and a teaspoonful of flour, and let it cook fifteen minutes. Salt meat can be cooked in the same way, omiting the salt; in its place put a small spoonful of sugar, spices or pickles, chopped fine, dish it on to some ship biscuit. Steaks, chops, sausages, bacon, or slices of any kind of meat can be cooked in a frying pan, with a little melted fat at the bottom. Salt meat should always be soaked.

www.ingramcontent.com/pod-product-compliance
Lightning Source LLC
Chambersburg PA
CBHW021442090426
42739CB00009B/1600